A LIVING ROOM JOURNEY

A LIVING ROOM JOURNEY

POEMS

Gerald Wallerstein

IPBOOKS.net
Infinite Possibilities

Infinite Possibilities
New York • http://www.IPBooks.net

Published by IPBooks,
Queens, NY 2022
Online at: www.IPBooks.net

First Edition

Cover design and interior layout by Noel S. Morado
Author's photo on the cover by Phyllis Wallerstein

ISBN 978-1-969031-06-9

For queries: coolguyj25@gmail.com

Contents

A Living Room Journey

An operation kept me off my feet for several months. I sat all day in my living room and seldom even climbed the stairs to sleep. The farthest I traveled was to the front steps of my house, except for once-a-week taxi rides to the surgeon's office. I was growing old but didn't want to feel elderly; the two words had different meanings for me; one was acceptable, the other less so. I observed as much as possible, without, I hoped, judgment.

I began to read, idly at first, but then I settled on Chinese, Japanese and Korean poetry. Almost all of my reading was of poets who wrote from twenty-five hundred to fifteen hundred years ago. I read Basho, the Han Shan poets, Ryokan, Li Po, Lu Yu, Soseki, Saigyo, Meng Chiao, Confucius, Rexroth's translations, Pound's translations. The struggle to understand my nature continued in my living-room. I hoped it was not too selfish a task. I leaned on other writers, such as Descartes and Pascal, from whom I took more comfort: they told me it was proper to sit alone in a room and think about myself. (And Frank O'Hara: "It is the law of my own voice I shall investigate.").

I was struck by Basho's *Narrow Road to the Deep North*, a record of one of his journeys. Wherever he went, he wrote poems, some haiku, some tanka. I could not travel. He and his companion even wrote poems on walls. Saigyo did the same. Instead, I journeyed in my house. In the present, I journeyed backward. The wonderful part of reading the ancient poems was that so many poems immediately struck a chord in my own memory.

I learned that the ancient poems I was reading were highly structured, though much of the formal qualities could not be maintained in translation. Once, though, I found a photograph of an ancient poem. The ideographs seemed to have been written on wood; they streamed down the page in a torrent of symbols. I thought: that's what a poem ought to look like, it ought to look as if it had been poured onto paper. I tried to copy the ancients in one respect only: commenting on my own poems.

I could not translate, paraphrase, copy or try to maintain any of the forms or the rules employed by the ancients. I did not try to create versions of any poem I read. The most I could do was use a phrase, a word, to bring forth recollections.[1] As I read, I began to travel, here, there, past, present and, dangerously, future. As Meng Chiao wrote, sorrow "blurs us and the ancients together." But memories are enjoyable in their own right, whether of sorrow or happiness, so every night I went in a different direction, without a goal, except perhaps to escape the room in which I sat. After a while I didn't want to escape. The ancients were concerned with the dilemmas I had faced: what to do for myself; what to do for others; what is absence; what is presence. The never-ending question of what I had accomplished? What do I remember and why do I remember it now? Longing for solitude, they also longed to be back in service. Most of these poems were written while sitting in that chair or on my front step. I was not suffering. The inability to remember, that is suffering.

---

1 Basho frequently placed phrases from Saigyo's poems into his own to ensure they would live on. LaFleur, p. 70.

A Mocking Comment by a Colleague

I spent my professional life analyzing
the weaknesses in the legal arguments
of adversaries, the habits of judges,
my own cleverness. Everything
depended on nuance and my nose
was always black from rubbing it with
ink-stained fingers. A colleague said
to me once: "You trust what you see
out of the corner of your eye more
than what you see in front of you."
I worried about that for a long time.
Tonight, when I crawled outside
to watch the new moon, I saw a slim
yellow crescent low in the Southwest.
I felt no dread at the late hour, or the passing
of time, or my gray hairs, or the mockery
of my colleague. I watched that crescent
until it sank in the west behind the roofs
across the way, until I was certain
my colleague had been wrong.

GERALD WALLERSTEIN

A Difficult Adversary

I was once a scholar in the law. I wrote important legal briefs, tried cases in the courts and won more than I lost.

I learned how to oppose my adversaries with integrity and fairness. Yet, when the doctor said I had to give up tobacco,

I went home, cried like a baby and caused my wife misery with my bitterness. No longer in public life, I had made an adversary

of myself. All I could do was complain. As I grow older I may grow up as well, but which will happen first, I can't say.

I have no argument to make about it, no court to which I might appeal.

After Lu Yu

I hardly know myself after all these years. My few friends would have to describe me. They might mention my broken, bent nose, my hairless scalp and my love of alcohol.

I would agree with them if what they said sounded accurate, but there are a few things they may not know: how it feels to smoke

a cigarette on a snowy night, to watch it disappear in a white bank without a sound, to hear the crackling of the icicles falling

from the eaves of the school across the street. If they don't know these things, they'll have missed my substance.

Still, I'll mutter their names between the Shéma and my last breath.

Wanting

This city has few pine trees,
no mountain caves,
hardly any serenity; how
will we find the right path with
all this noise, all these bricks?
Must we hold open
the Gate for everyone,
unable to look inside
until they've all gone in?
If we're doomed to keep
wanting, isn't that what
we ought to want? Isn't it?

An Unwanted Question

I wanted to live a long life, at least to seventy-five, a year longer
than my father's span. Now, laid up, hobbling about on crutches,

I gaze out my window day and night. The sun and moon hardly mingle
with our narrow street and its deep shadows. I can't see

the stars for all the tall buildings. I sit in my chair and ponder: why am
I competing with a ghost?

Distractions

As I write in my room, one lamp lit behind me, our eighteen-year old
cat, who has lost her mind and howls during the night,

has come to beg for food. I get out of my chair putting aside pen and
paper, to go into the kitchen and fill her bowl. She trots

over to it, sniffs, and walks back to the living room, indignant, to howl
again. I want to give her a strong lecture for wasting my

time and taking me away from my writing, but I get to imagining a
Chinese poet a thousand years ago who had to get up

in the middle of a winter's night to go to the well outside only to find
when he got back to his hut that all the water had run out from a hole
in his bucket.

He'd been so intrigued by the sound made by his sandals on the wet
snow that he hadn't noticed the leak. It seemed only right

after that to listen more carefully to the cat's howling, the rise and fall
of it, her valid complaint, while I opened another can and set fresh food
on the floor.

Mother's Hands

At the end of her life, my mother lay in
bed, her hands moving over the covers.
I watched her pick lint off the quilt
and drop the pieces over the edge to
the floor. Now, no longer in public
life, I sit quietly in my room,
my hands unable to be still. They see
the future before I do. They move on
their own while there's still time.

GERALD WALLERSTEIN

The Problem With Reading At Night

I fell asleep reading Descartes' *Treatise on Method,* with his rules for thought, his balance of reason and intuition. Startled

by a noise, I woke up and read a poem of Wang-An- Shih, who says *"[i]n dream, emperors Yao and Chieh sometimes appear,*

one noble, one vile." In the morning I recalled a dream: an old bald man leaned over a young man saying *'She's gone, you have*

to get over it.' And I'd been thinking of two women as I read that night, but I didn't know which one the old man meant. Both had rejected me.

Then Descartes told me it wouldn't matter, and Wang-An-Shih said a dream which presents a choice always ends in grief.

Black fingernails

Today I planted impatiens, white along the border, orange
in the center of the plot, patted down the dirt, watered,

sat on my steps with alcohol and a cigarette, looked at my
fingernails, black with potting soil, pants caked with dirt.

I felt like a dynamo, though my happiness exists in a void,
with no one but the plants to see it. Still, it's good to feel

like a dynamo. Who can speak accurately of his own birth?
What's given is the means to describe our many rebirths.

The ancients had no dynamos, but they knew how I felt.

[Spring came; I was still unable to walk much but I could put some
weight on my injured foot. I hobbled out to the florist's shop nearby
and asked the owner to carry some plants to our house. That afternoon
I composed this poem.]

GERALD WALLERSTEIN

Cold Mountain, Warm Steps

The Han Shan poets who lived in isolation
on Cold Mountain - did they know I'd be
reading their poems a thousand years later?
Tonight I made coffee for the vagrants and
workers who pass by late. I sat on my
step waiting for someone to come along.
No one came but my preparations
were satisfying. In the city, I gazed at the
same moon the old poets saw. It's my
companion, too, after all. And they weren't
as alone as they would have us believe;
even the waning moon kept company.

Song of A Dry Winter

It was good of you
to lock up the spirits
and hide the key.

You've always taken
good care of me, no one
knows that more than I do.

But my knees ache,
and I can't leave the
house in this weather.

You know I've given up
wine, and you're my only
woman; I certainly can't
sing worth a damn.

So here, just take this eyedropper.
Put a drop of rum on my tongue.
Just one drop, for me.

Do it every night, won't you?
It's so damned cold,
and April, April is so far away.

GERALD WALLERSTEIN

Freight Train At Night

The old man's aware of himself
as he walks down the street.
He's a prowling wolf with
a scowl on his face, or a
slithering snake with hooded eyes.
Keep away! his body says.
And everyone does. One night
he hears the mournful horn
of a freight train moving through
a cut to the Northwest; then
he knows he's neither lupine
nor reptilian. There's little
worth keeping away. Every
sound's a fanfare, a mother,
a father, youth. He walks on,
his spine, muscles, sinew
working together. *Fiat homo!,*
said the train. *Fiat homo!*

goddamned Cricket

I waited all summer for the goddamned cricket to arrive
as one seems to do every summer in September and it was
already August I could imagine the first bitter breezes
about to come There was nothing I could do about it so
I talked to the nine flowering maples across the street,
their branches raised to the sky but not in prayer
because my speech was about how you cannot
be too religious and still be a citizen in a republic, not if
God is always talking to you and you are talking back I
didn't even want to give him or her or it a capital G but
I respect the idea though I've never met him or her or it
If I'm going to wait for anything it'll be that goddamned
cricket, not armageddon or the rapture I'd rather give
my capital letters to the Cricket He's the one who comes
sooner or later and he's musical, too Anyway both
of us are goddamned and we're alright with it We'll
make our own music when he shows up

GERALD WALLERSTEIN

On Being A Good Host

I've used too many words without knowing their meanings.
Talking's become more difficult as I listen to myself with more care.

How could I ever make a friend in a world with so many words?
Han Shan writes *"No one's talk makes perfect harmony with mine"*.

Come sit with me, quietly. No need to talk. I'll be in harmony with you;
in discord with myself, but in harmony with you.

Heaven, Satori

Books, poems, everywhere in the house;
highways toward the self, away from the
self. At night, in his chair, he wants to
forget he's ever heard the words:
Heaven Satori Bliss. Lost in November,
he hopped outside for a cigarette.
The cat on the pavement stopped
in mid-prowl, bony, dirty, colorless
gray; filth. It stared at him, he stared
back, until it disappeared under a car.
Then, he gave up his sense, asked himself:
if a homeless man would have stared;
would he have gazed back? He caught
himself thinking *That's the beginning
of all kinds of trouble. That's the first
step toward Heaven, toward Satori.*
He wants to be a Mahayana. He'd
hold open the Kingdom's door for
everyone in the world before he'd
dare to look inside. It's hard to live
that way now. He couldn't live
any other; he tries, but it's hard.
He's unsure of himself. He's done
too much reading.

Older Heroes

A useless action that contributes to the tranquility of the world
is nonetheless heroic.
If I recline in my chair with the nineteen-year-old tortoiseshell
splayed across my thighs,
if I put down my novel to count the whitish whiskers sprouting from
each side of her nose,
if I count twelve from the left side, fifteen from the right,
if our eyes meet, our pupils contract under the light from the
table lamp, could anything be more useless?
The Japanese writer whose book I've put aside says
"Tranquility never comes to the self-mocking man." And Lu Yu says: *"White
hairs have no power to dampen the mood I'm in."*
I say we are heroes. In that chair, we've made an *us*.

Japan

The greatest of the Japanese novelists
often spend a paragraph or two describing
their own witlessness, even stupidity.
It seems a necessary introduction,
a symbolic honor to the reader,
a self-imposed humility. Yet,
a few pages later, we are presented
with a kitchen, two women
chopping onions or carrots
on a cutting board, the soft lilt
of their voices, their worry
about the unmarried daughter-
it is the older, married daughter
in the kitchen with her mother -
while the father, who has always
been distant and who has become
haughtier with age and misunderstanding,
walks among the Pauwlonia trees
in the back garden, which, for thirty years
have acted as the windbreak he intended
when he first planted them. We read on,
looking for the heart of things
and we see it is there in the onions,
the quiet voices, the sharp knife,
the old man who cannot admit to anyone

his misery, who putters through the trees
which, in a short time, will no longer
keep out the wind. We've been there
all along. The rest is gloss.

Honor

In my analyst's waiting room I spoke
to a whore who was also a patient.
She said *My Christian clients*
are the cheapest, the Catholics better,
but the Jews are the most generous.
Later I visited her in the apartment
where she saw her clients. The closet
was full of designer dresses and expensive
shoes. I left thinking *Some honors are*
dubious, but honor's honor, how
generous my people are with our totems.

Hullabaloo

Sitting on a bench in the park next to the art school.
Other older men, two dogs, a woman who never
looks at anyone. I've counted thirteen trees, sturdy,
in full leaf; another woman walking a pinscher asks me
how I'm doing. I'm living in the moment, I say,
after thinking about it, no thought of Japanese poets,
or Lu Yu. I'm not doing anything else, am I?
Nothing to do but get rid of some anxiety. The park: a
hullabaloo for old men and women. Later, fireworks
across town. I'll see them from my third-floor room.

The Thought Had Stayed Within Me For A Long Time Until Blood Brought It Out

I hopped into the kitchen and
cut my finger washing knives
in the sink. Blood pulsed out
and I screamed but no one heard.
I almost fainted. It's an accurate
account, with no meaning, no
explanation. Only blood. A lot
of blood. I hopped back to my
chair and fell backward into it.
Only then could I laugh. I told
no one what had happened. I'd
have been warned: no more
hopping! Now I hop when
everyone's gone to bed, my
fingers and my cleverness
still intact.

GERALD WALLERSTEIN

An Imp In the Night Sky

For three nights I stepped outside around midnight to find
the waning moon low in the West. Tonight I looked again

and it wasn't there. I thought of the few friends I have left.
I know they're around, but I can't always find them. I have

to go looking for them, just like that teasing moon. I think
they're all tricksters, the moon, too. All the same I'm less alone

knowing they're somewhere. I can wait. It's good to have
company even if it plays hide-and-seek with me.

Justification

In my room one lamp is lit,
two cats are fighting for my lap.
Through the window the moon
begs my attention.
My necessity surprises me.

GERALD WALLERSTEIN

Letters

Writers and artists die and their correspondence
Is published. Hundreds, thousands of letters.
Van Gogh, Dostoievski. I pretend to be a Russian
Novelist living in isolation. A small dacha.
I spend my money gambling. I miss every deadline.
I'm anxious all the day long.
Anushka cooks and sweeps and groans quietly
but I pay no attention. I know I'm not a very
good man and it causes me anguish, but I think only
of writing letters: *Dear Mischa, how are you,*
God willing you are in good health and writing.
Masha is fine but gets little from me, certainly
not in the way of money. I pray you and I
will meet in St. Petersburg this year. We'll
stroll the Nevsky Prospekt and drink wine.
I want to hear everything from you!
I miss our friendship. I pray for both of us.
Your devoted friend, -----." Letters come
more from my heart than books. My own
correspondence will never see daylight.

Making An Axe

For Gary Snider

I should learn how to grow old
and do it well. Tomorrow I lunch
with friends, one's eighty, the other's
eighty-five. Lu Ji and Ezra Pound
both said *"When making an axe
with an axe, the model is not
far off"*. I'll stay close to my friends,
no matter how things turn out.

My Life

I explain myself to myself
over and over,
the voice forever childish,
as a cocky ten-year old speaks
to a naïve seven-year old,
using small words.
This is how you ride a bicycle.
This is how you dig a hole.
Neither child knows much.
I am still digging holes,
planting seeds. I am still naïve,
still cocky. Each year
my plot grows smaller,
less fertile. My confidence
is foolish but, at the same time,
astonishing.

Old Man In His Room

Old man in his room with three cats. He's recalling
his past ferocities, examining his general history
of meanness, still guarding his suspicions. The cats'
pleading frightens him as they fight for his lap.
He lets one jump up, grudgingly, strokes it gently.
Even his gentleness frightens him. *Is there a way*
he thinks, *that comes without struggle, without*
knowing it's come? If something creeps up
behind you, is it always terrible?

GERALD WALLERSTEIN

On A Train With Lu Yu Traveling Through New Jersey

On the train to New York,
going to the Kandinsky exhibit
at the Guggenheim, thinking of
mother and father, long gone,
friends old and ill. We race
through flatland: bare trees,
gray sky, a few circling hawks.
Now we know that the land races
by us, too. I wonder if Einstein
will be the only one of us known
in a thousand years?
As we know Ptolemy?
Or Copernicus? Who
of us will leave behind
what Lu Yu calls
*"the fragrance of a
good name"?* Pleasantly,
the train rocks us forward.
At the Museum
I'll see swaths of color,
yellow, green, earth tones,
the early Kandinsky,
before he took up geometry.

On the Uselessness of Certain Presumptions

Once I found my footing as a lawyer
I always presumed that my clients
would take my advice. Now that I'm
retired, I go to the doctor and squirm
like an unruly child when he tells me
what to do. He doesn't ask about
my experience, my expertise.
We aren't peers. I end up thinking
I should have asked the carpenter
about mortises and tenons and the
housewife about finances. They
might have listened to me.

GERALD WALLERSTEIN

Two Poets

Our obese cat sleeps all day. At night he waddles downstairs
to steal the food I put down for our other cats. He has no values.

It's because of him I write against my own grain,
restless and amoral as I am in my chair in the dark living room.

Paths

All this worry about the right path;
such a burden! The freight train
passing through a cut has found its
right path. The cigarette arcing
into the snow on a cold night has
found its right path. The lost
traveler finds the right path.
Every line of thought is the
right path. A deliberate
grammatical error is sometimes
necessary. It, too, is the right path.
I'll never be done with desire
and greed. If what I say is right,
they're also the right path.

Rothko

Terry Rolland, a painter I knew in the '70's,
explained Rothko to me one evening over
dinner. "Imagine a landscape under a sky.
Now, take away the landscape." I can't
say whether she was right; I'm not a painter.
But as I grow older I begin to see
the implications of her explanation.
My own landscape was fuzzy to
begin with; now I can hardly make it out.
It's as if Rothko was painting dying in
the most appropriate colors, earth tones,
with a few reds, some orange. His own
landscape was missing from the start.
As I say, though, I'm not a painter.

Sensei

For Jack

O fat orange cat throwing off flecks of dandruff
everywhere, what has roused you from the sopor
of your Zappo's box on the third floor? Why have
you hurtled yourself downstairs to the living room
where I was asleep on the sofa having written until
it was too late to climb the stairs to bed without
waking my wife? My right leg is bent at the knee,
my left is crossed over it. I fell asleep using my
left thumb-the only one with a decent nail-to saw
off a long toenail. The food bowls are in the kitchen
but you have come to wake me at four thirty in the
morning to tell me, without pretense, that everything
is unified. Now I am awake; still a student, with much
silliness and fear to answer for, but awake! It is good
to live with a Zen master. I will grapple with these
things. I think we'll come to terms.

Shallow Snow

Shallow snow on the street; underneath,
a hard layer of ice, but I can't smoke in
the house. Outside, a young woman is
starting her car, the rear wheels spinning,
rubber burning. I shout:
"Put it in gear; let it drive itself" but she
doesn't hear me-her windows are up.
Finally, off she goes! fishtailing up the
street. She didn't need my help.
Now I'm under my quilt again.
I've met the world on its own terms,
mine, too.

Sitting

When the ancient Zen poets wrote of *sitting*, they meant *meditating*. Whether they sat in a hut, or at the edge of a pond, or in a chair gazing from the only window of a hovel with a dirt floor, they weren't *merely* sitting. They hadn't read Aristotle, who'd have told them: *"When I sit, I sit; when I meditate, I meditate."*

The Interior

I woke from a dream in which the Emperor of Burkina Faso sat slumped on a folding chair in native garb, wearing a headdress of wild bird feathers.

A line of tourists sat in chairs behind him. It was impossible to know its meaning, but how vast the place from whence it came!

And how colorful! I'd go there, but where to book passage?

Mirrors

The novel I wrote nineteen years ago was my life story,
(though I changed all the names and locations).

Now, when I'm at a party or on the sidewalk, a face or a sound
brings back what I wrote, more than what actually happened.

I have two sets of memories, reflecting mirrors
placed opposite one another. Incomplete, I live between them,

waiting for that which really happened and how I described it
to clasp hands in friendship and resolve their differences.

Balance

The painter's coming tomorrow; after him,
the window installer.

We'll choose bright living-room colors
and extra-dense storm windows;

thick panes to keep the cold air out and the warm air in.
It took us a long time to make these choices.

In the end we decided we wanted to be comfortable
while we read and studied.

Housekeeping and learning stem from the same root.
A house knows this right away; it took us longer.

Full Price

We paid for every item without argument
over cost. Automobiles, refrigerators,
our son's education. We never learned
how to bargain, and we joked that we
were the only Jews who didn't buy
wholesale. When death comes I'll
have no argument to make. I'll have
to pay full price, with no discount.

History

We fade away like so many dewdrops on green leaves,
but for a time we were bathed in sunlight.

(Every time the sun rises and sets it is writing our obituaries.).

What Will I Do?

Lying in bed, gray hair on a white pillow, watching snow fall,
warm under my quilt. What will I do when I'm dying?

Our son's grown, my wife has her wits about her.
It's likely I'll lie in bed, quilted as I am now,

until drowsiness overtakes me, wondering
if I've done enough, letting it be alright if I haven't.

Loss

When I was young and working I came home each night and fell on my bed for an hour or two. Every work-day took something away and left a piece over here, over there.

While I rested I looked for what I'd lost. Then I'd eat supper at ten o'clock, read, fall asleep with what I'd been able to recover. In the morning I'd go back to work.

Over time, not as much came back in the evenings. I couldn't replace the restless parts; I thought they were the most important ones. Now I sit quietly, looking from my window

to the trees across the way, bathed in moonlight. What they lose returns after three phases of the moon, with no effort, without care.

Whole

It's too late for any of us
to be whole
too much damage
has been done
We can't work at it
the world divides our
attention into fourths,
eighths, sixteenths
Separate pieces floating
In the seas of our lives
must find their own
harmony without
our help
Yet, tonight, at 3:30 am,
standing on my step
with vodka and a cigarette
I heard a freight-train whistle
as it ran through a cut
and I slept well, as if
I'd been to a museum
that afternoon, or
watched fireworks
light up the night sky.

Fresh Air

Will you please lie down in a dark room?
Talk to yourself. Say anything you like.
You needn't say it out loud, just whisper it,
or think it.

Imagine someone's sitting near you, silent.
He wouldn't say much anyway.

After a while you'll see you've taken his place.
You'll hear yourself, and you'll be him, too,
listening. You'll be two listeners
and one speaker.

See how it goes. Keep it up.
When the ghosts begin to hover near the ceiling
you'll know they came to listen, too.
They'll want to hear what you're saying.
They'll hear you, you'll hear yourself;
all of you will atone, strangely.
not for what you've done
but for what's been done to you.

You'll all come to some kind of understanding,
but you'll do it without compromising too much.
That's fair, isn't it? That's just.

It's what all of you wanted; not everything
you wanted, but enough. Enough
is often quite a lot.

Get up, then, step outside. Breathe.
Tomorrow, do it again.
The ghosts may still be there. That's alright.
They came outside with you, didn't they?
Fresh air's good for them. When
you return to that dark room,
the air follows you; it wants to know you
better, all of you

A Table

There was a time I felt as if I lived in one of the Eastern Bloc countries
and not America; that was when I called my father one night from my
flat after I'd had a few drinks and asked him
if he loved Communism more than he loved me and he said *yes*
without hesitating, though to be honest he hadn't wanted to get
on the phone but I insisted, and in a way I felt liberated,
as I thought a young man in Eastern Europe would where
the worst truth is still true and might provide a small breath
of freedom. A few weeks later my father came to my flat with
two bags of groceries which I certainly needed and after
he climbed three flights of steps I told him to fuck off
and he left with the groceries and I thought I was a little freer.
A few weeks after that he made me a table in his cellar shop
out of birchwood which is one of the hardest woods
and he carried that table up the same three flights of steps and
this time I let him in. He stood on the table and jumped
up and down on it to show me how strong it was; it was very strong and
he left and I kept the table. We were thinking alike for once; we wanted
to be free but not too free. Hard words had been spoken but the table
was harder and we had said too much anyway.

With Persistence, Without Explanation

Newspaper delivery boy,
gas station attendant,
factory worker, cab driver,
civilian clerk for the Army,
employee of the state,
municipal employee, now
I collect two pensions and
one social security check
(on the fourth Wednesday
of each month). All of it
prepared me to sit in my
room and think. None of it
was Karma, none of it
made me blessed. I was
only another citizen.
I stare into a mirror
without a single question
to ask. No sense blaming
anyone. Blame only
interferes with pondering,
the last job I expect I'll have.
Meng Chiao says:
Invariably pure and austere,
poets mostly starve to death
embracing empty mountains.

All in all, it's good that I don't
write many poems now.
As bad artists continue to paint,
I continue to live,
with persistence, without
explanation.

Autumn

Sitting on his front step
watching leaves fall,
pondering in silence,
he stumbles to the
pavement and hits
his head. He climbs
back up the steps,
thinking: "*Leaves never
cry 'Help me!' as they
hit the ground.*" He's
fallen into unity with
nature by accident, that is,
the correct way.

Without Arrogance

Stroking the cat on my lap thoughtlessly,
I realized I wasn't paying her any attention.

I suddenly wondered what would happen
if I saw everything as a unity.

Then I thought: a true Buddha would go
back to the not-seeing right away; that

would be real oneness. It is like cleaning
one's house; it ought to be done again

and again. Then you are alongside
everyone; you see how hard it is not
to strive.

Persistence of Infantility

An old man should know the difference
between what is possible and what is not.
He was born into impossibility. The breast
wasn't always available. Mama often
left the room for a minute. Father
couldn't explain. Impossibility led to
bitterness and curiosity, two streams
which course through every life,
sometimes meeting, sometimes not.
Now he sits in his chair, comfortable,
taking the long view, having endured,
having straddled both streams, now dry.
Still, he remembers the names of every
woman he ever slept with, which he
savors along with the alcohol in the
glass beside the chair, the tobacco
in his pipe.

Nighttime

Lu Yu at seventy with his ten thousand poems,
riding on a donkey, wondering why he's a poet
and not back in government service overthrowing
invaders from the North. Making sure his
eighty-five compilations are saved. Stendhal writing
the Charterhouse of Parma in six weeks. His Life
of Henri Brulard with diagrams of his childhood
home. "I write for a hundred readers", he says.
I ought to turn off my lamp, but insistent
geese are flying northwest over the house
to the riverbank where they spend the summer.
"Keep the light on! Keep the light on!"
How good it would be if they were speaking
on behalf of Lu Yu and Stendhal! But that's
impossible. Still, I go to the kitchen to boil
water for coffee. Going in the wrong
direction, as the geese were.

(I've hedged my own bet against mortality,
laying off the odds after a hot tip from
a flock of flying touts.)

Tired of Reading the Ancient Poets, I Turn to the Analects to Learn About Right Conduct

I've turned off my lamp but the bulb is still hot, and the darkness inside is attuned to the dark without. I'd been reading the Analects. How to live a moral life. How to follow the right precepts. Two thousand years of thought: who has rights? Who has obligations? All the ancients concerned with proper conduct, all the while knowing the child within will sometimes have his way. A large moth flits past the strip of light coming from the street lamp toward the hot bulb, away, then back again. I pick up the folded newspaper from the table beside my chair. If I can stun it, I'll wrap it in paper and push it through the open window. I swipe at it, catching one fluttering wing; it falls to the floor. It struggles to raise itself as I slide the paper under it. All that happens is that I push it farther away from me. It continues to struggle but now it's too far away to slide the paper beneath it. I think of the Analects as I raise the newspaper over the moth and smash it to the floor. There was nothing in the Analects that covered the situation I faced. Or, if there was, I skipped over it. Poor moth, it kept me in the world of things at great cost.

War Poem

"Even the pines that remain unaffected
are lonely on the peak." Tsurayuki

The woman who is neither old nor young
carries branches for kindling down the hill
toward the village, stepping carefully
over ruts and around boulders. When the
kindling falls, she stops, bends, picks it up.
The men sitting outside the tavern watch her
with indifference as they talk of what they did
in the war. One says "courage isn't something
you have all the time, it comes and goes..."
Another says "Or never comes at all".
Laughter. The woman bends again
to adjust her bundle, the men's words,
their laughter, pass over her
to the pine trees on the hill,
which remain serene, unaffected.

———————————————

(I wrote this poem before I found a line
from a poem by Tsurayuki, which ends:
"Even the pines that remain unaffected,
are lonely on the peak." On the other
hand, every field of flowers in the world
has been covered by blood and brains
at one time or another. Arboretums
remind me only of slaughter. Hedgerows,
too.)

Combination of The Two

"Why" is for the rationalists, who wonder why they haven't really lived. And I gave my own definitions to words; tragedy: when the quality you value the most causes your downfall; and Irony: when what you try to do turns out to cause the exact opposite of what you intended. This train of thoughts got me thinking about a time on the subway when the man next to me blew smoke in my face. He said "Find another seat if you don't like it" and I couldn't let it go with the two young girls across the aisle watching and listening, so I took the biggest book from my briefcase and raised it over my head, then brought it down with a swoop on the man's hands and the cigarette between his fingers. He jumped up and took one swing at me, which broke my nose. I spent a week in the hospital until the arterial bleeding stopped. Two moments of joy: running from the subway to my office, proud I had stood up for myself, and watching the faces of my parents as the doctor finally pulled the pack from my nose and blood spurted out with me so full of Demerol all I could do was laugh. Those girls-I couldn't let them see my weakness-I couldn't let them see that I *thought* I was weak. In the end, they must have thought I was an idiot. Yet it's hard for me to go back to that rationalism. It's something to do with that Janis Joplin song, "Combination of the Two". It takes a fool to put some things together, irony; tragedy. Sometimes you have to be a fool, and then you think you've lived, you know you've lived.

Evil

In Hebrew School we drew swastikas on the blackboard
when our teacher went to the men's room, erasing them
after we heard the flushing of the toilet. We brought
bags of French fries covered in salt to the classroom,
munched on them while we learned the alphabet.
Bernie Skoboloff brought a spare tire to the class,
parked it on the seat next to his. We didn't think
we were doing anything wrong. We didn't think
we were mocking anyone. We may have felt
ashamed, but not evil. The other night I sent
off a manuscript to a contest, pulled a book from the shelf:
The Destruction of the European Jews. As I read,
I imagined my manuscript being pulled from a train,
lined up with a thousand others; I saw the judge
raise his hand toward each: *That one to the left,*
this one to the right-it looks strong enough
to work. The ones on the left would go up
in smoke, the ones on the right would live
for a while. I'd always thought of evil
as overt, visible in action, not simple
as a train of thought, sitting in one's chair,
equating one's striving with that to which
it ought never to be compared.

Friends

I was explaining the meaning of life one Friday night
to Al Ferrari in the Pine Street Beverage Room
while he drank his way through almost a case of beer
because he was driving across the River later to see a woman
in New Jersey whom he'd only talked to over the phone
and if she turned out to be ugly he wanted to see
that ugliness through a haze, but someone shoved me
and I shoved back-it was very crowded-
and I had shoved a bouncer who picked me up and
carried me to the front door with my feet never touching
the floor and told me to get out and stay out. Al
had to come with me before he finished his beer. When he
came back from New Jersey he never told me what happened
with the woman but I know that before he went to bed
he stole a 'For Sale' sign near the Bridge
and replanted it on the lawn of a neighbor he hated,
probably pounding it into the grass with an empty beer can.
It wasn't a bad life; we came out of it with stories to tell.
I wish I could remember what I said to him that night.
It was something about how the part of our brain that listens
is always judging the part of our brain that thinks and
that's where the trouble lies. I was talking to myself
as well as to Al, but we were both too drunk to listen.
It had seemed to make a lot of sense.
We were friends and whooped it up for a time; but
we had to be satisfied with knowing we had only been
close to something great, that even if we had forgotten it,
we had our chance to know it, once.

Kiss

How wonderful is
that first kiss! Yet,
if before your lips
touch hers, a thought
comes: *Why*
should I be loved?,
everything's already
gone to hell, and you
will remember the
question instead of
the kiss, which flew
away as a startled
bird rises to a
sharp noise.
Oh, it might be just me!
When I see a bird, I
think *'bird'!* and I
become restless,
without purpose.

Reading Bei Dao

As we moved my taciturn son from
his dormitory in June I dug through
his trash to find the A+ papers
he'd thrown away. I didn't want them
to be lost, but he surprised me
with a gift, the poems of Bei Dao.

Later, I read them with difficulty.
They were terse, full of zig-zags,
jumps, turns, allusions.

I had to read them again
in a soft chair, with the
fourteen-year old brindle cat on my lap;
until I began to understand.

The cat does not know she will die;
Bei Dao does, as will his words,
if they stop moving. He's sent them
to us for safekeeping.

Bei Dao writes *"This is you,*
this is you, pressed upon
by fleeting shadows..."

When I stood up, the cat wondered:
"Where did his lap go." Both of us
ought to get moving, I thought.

Next year, I'll dig again through
the trash of my son's dorm room.
Everything must be saved, every
word.

A Kind of Reciprocity

Whenever he thought of suicide he explained to himself
that suffering has form and function like any thing
and can be manipulated. The explanation comforted
him because he didn't think he wanted to die; he was
afraid something unknown would spring forth from
his insides before he could control it. His talking
to himself made him more alert. It got him thinking,
too, about the young suicidal writer he'd met,
who'd already written two novels about her own
suffering. He'd explained to her how he dealt with
the idea while they sat drinking coffee. He'd told her
she could get another ten years out of just thinking
about what he'd said. When he'd finished she slapped
him full on in the face. For a month or so he read
the papers and didn't find any mention of her;
he thought *"Now we're both alert"* He hoped he'd done
a good thing, though he worried about the brutality
of it. He wondered what she'd have thought if
he'd slapped her instead, decided she'd not have
minded if it had helped *him.* And he'd have done it
out of love. Her slap had been out of love, too;
she just didn't know it, yet.

GERALD WALLERSTEIN

Exupery

He was trying to write about love, couldn't find
the right words, wasn't sure who he was writing
to. Outside, he smoked, listened for the
cricket who began late every night; no sound;
even the passing cars were quiet. Gray clouds
raced above, the tail end of a storm, breaking
up into black, amoebic gaps, stars like pearls
on velvet gleamed and quickly disappeared.
He thought then of Exupery looking down
through those gaps, a quilt of lights below,
a skein of stars above. He thought there
must always be a *middle, an in-between.*
He continued to smoke, feeling better,
not knowing exactly why.

———————————————————

(When Saigyo watches the clouds break to let him see the moon he
longed for, he calls it *"a storm that knows compassion"*).

My Father And I And Pascal

Father, you were not so good.
Your tyranny frightened me
when I had no strength.
And what did I
find in your wallet but the
quote that was my patrimony?
The eternal silence of these
infinite spaces frightens me.
The same man said *All of*
man's troubles arise from
his inability to sit alone
in his room. I tried that,
and yet you are still with me.
I miss you warily.
Is it that way for you, too?

Legacy

He was a communist
She was a housewife
From them I took

Rebel! Adjust!
Suffer! Endure!
Praxis! Be still!
You *must know!* Who knows?

He always said *After laughing
comes crying.* All her life she
said *We'll see... We'll see.*

He willed me a thesis
She willed me an antithesis.

I am no synthesis
I know nothing of dialectics.

Sometimes, I just stand still
and shiver until I get hungry
or tired. Then I move on.

If I live a hundred years
I'll never be able to spend
what they left me.

Pall

Always in the flat a pall of cigarette smoke.
Uncles who lived nearby popping in for coffee;
too many political discussions; McCarthy did this,
Eisenhower did that, five-year plans, Aunt Florence
naming her dogs after Lenin's wife and Stalin's daughter.
And the waking in the middle of the night covered
with overcoats. Do you see what I am getting at?
What to do for you? What to do for me? My only novel
sits unfinished. It became more of a Talmud
than a story. If I had rules, I thought,
I could live without a pall. I wanted to tell everyone
how to live, too. I didn't know how easy
it would have been to point my chin upward
toward the ceiling, to blow the smoke away.
I was eight years old, already too old.

A Dream

...Had two piles of old clothes
Put them in garbage bags
Propped the bags up against a dumpster
in a parking lot
Looked like two homeless persons sleeping
top heavy, barrel-chested, thin legs
Couldn't sit up straight
Went to a mall Came back with two shopping bags
My homeless persons hadn't moved
Filled the bags with the clothes Came away
Hoped I hadn't been seen
Dad was a Communist... believed in praxis
Mom was a housewife... believed in endurance
He was in my left hand, she in my right
Had to be them, all right
In that lot, my right hand loosened its grip
Good-bye, mom!
I knew you'd persevere
I knew he'd have to be carried
The bag I kept was heavier but I held on
It needed a home
I think I'll never get rid of him
Not as long as I live
I think I don't want to
Why else would I hold onto that bag so tightly?
The macadam under my feet
was humming a marching song

It could have been *The Marseillaise*
or *The Internationale*
I'm sure it was one or the other
It paced my steps
as if it were a throbbing heart
The mind, doing its work;
two angry men going home.

River-Wide

I imagine sending poems to another poet as a gift.
I also imagine his reply: *"I don't like them"*, he says.
"I don't like them at all. The last two lines don't pull
the poems together. You hardly use adverbs
or adjectives. There's no meat in them and
there's no meaning either. You haven't
given us a story." He doesn't like them at all,
but he can't see that my smile is *river-wide*.

(A story of Po-Chu-Ih says he used to read his poems to a simple woman and, if she didn't understand them he rewrote them even more simply. Of course, we'll never know whether he saved some of the ones she didn't like without rewriting them.)

(Adjectives and similes were used sparingly, according to Cooper, but leaps in thought were welcomed.)

"No Comment"

When I lost a legal case reporters would
approach me with questions. I was even filmed
as I left the courthouse. I always said *"No
comment"*. My wife had been a reporter;
her advice-to say nothing more-was
excellent. But now I can go on the internet
and see how I looked when I spoke those
words. I hadn't read Wang–An–Shih's
request to a friend as he felt Autumn
coming on: *"[W]ho welcomes the worry
of this life. Let's go out, walking sticks
in hand, and gaze into all change itself"*.
I could have said that to the reporters;
I might even have made a friend. Now
I have two walking sticks, but no case
to argue, no courthouse to leave.

No Mountain

On the one hand, no mountain,
no cave, no hut, no flowers, no
pond, no frogs, no meditation.
On the other, a front step,
trees across the way,
pigeons, starlings, concrete,
traffic, full mind, stars.
What more would I need?
Oh! and the moon, waxing or
waning, makes no difference
to me.

A Miserable Winter

I sit in my chair at night with an empty urinal on the floor;
In the morning it's full and my wife carries it upstairs

to pour into the toilet. When she leaves I look into a mirror;
an unshaven, unkempt, unemployed man who's become uglier

than ever looks back at me. He's growing crabbier as the days
grow short and winter nears. Kenko writes that even if a woman

is beautiful and her husband of low birth, he may look down
on her all the same because of his own worthlessness. But I think:

*"Would any woman be likely to throw away her life on a
wretch like me?"* The worse I feel, the angrier I become

at the woman who cares for me; I ignore her lifelong
beauty. sunk in disgust for my own helplessness.

GERALD WALLERSTEIN

The Writer From The Written

The man reads poems all the time: journals, books,
chapbooks. He asks himself: what is being sought:
something-ness or nothingness? Bareness
or adornment? He loves most poets, knows
the work they put into it. Only a few
he won't read-the ones he believes were
antisemites, Pound, Eliot (though he cheats with Pound -
every line is so gorgeous). He's done the same
with novelists, Agatha Christie, Dorothy Sayers,
Bram Stoker, Edith Wharton. He knows
he should separate the writer
from the written (he'd like his readers –
if he has any-to follow the same rule).
Now he thinks about the Big Bang.
and why are the stars accelerating away from
one another? What does that mean
about the beginning of it all? There are
big puzzles and small ones, aren't there?
He sneaks back to Pound again, takes
another look at Eliot's *Wasteland*.
He ponders and decides not every puzzle
needs to be solved, not by him, anyway.

He wants to learn, even from people
who didn't like him or his kind. It's
a silent, gentle retaliation. He's chosen
bareness, something-ness, even if
they're just gloss over fury.

(The Analects teach: "A gentleman does not [A]ccept men because of
what they say, [N]or reject sayings, because the speaker is what he is).

A Fine Mist

A mist unworthy of being called a drizzle fell on the trees across the way. The birds quietly waited for dawn, the wind was too tired to move the branches. Stars waited for the clouds to break.

I 'd just read a line in an Italian crime novel: *"I have not betrayed my youth . . ."* and gone outside to smoke, disturbed .
I asked myself who I'd betrayed?

It was a very long list; I was young then and couldn't take the long view of anyone, nor myself. I thought

dad was a tyrant, mom a weakling. The woman I said I loved I lied to, the woman I said I didn't love I also lied to. That long view came too late.

How could I have lived without betrayal when I paid no attention to the accuracy of the words I spoke about myself and others?

So maybe it's best to betray only yourself if you know nothing of constancy. As I smoked I saw it for the first time, the fine mist, the patient birds,

branches hardly swaying. I'd betrayed them, too. At most, I felt I was little more than mist, little less than a drizzle, a bit, just a bit unnatural.

In the trees across the way, full-leafed
in October, starlings are carrying on their
own intrigues, perhaps dreaming of
romance, or victory, or compromise,
busier than I am, and noisier. The
nestlings whimper, as if they want
a bedtime story, warm milk, a
good-night peck.

Bang! Bang! Bang!

Margaret Levinson was a very good poet in a workshop I attended once, who did not get much recognition in her life, possibly because the subjects of her poems were elderly women, often Jewish, living out their remaining time in low-rent apartment buildings where the only recreation room was a fire escape opposite a wall of dirty brick, where lives might be relived for good or bad. Her poems, the ones she read in the workshop, were factual but preserved the dignity of her subjects, a talent I came to appreciate as I grew older and began to see with some dread what I might look forward to. Margaret knew how to praise simply by observation; that, too, is talent.

I had not thought much about Margaret since 1977, when I almost blinded her in one eye with a champagne cork in a meeting room of the Jewish Y on Broad Street in Philadelphia. I don't remember why we were drinking champagne-it might have been that one of our group had finally gotten a poem published, and I might have continued to forget her, at least continued to forget my gaucherie, had I not tried the other day to jam some books into an already-full bookshelf in our den. When the shelf collapsed, Margaret's chapbook fell onto the top of the pile. I had had it for over thirty years.

I sat down and began reading the chapbook, which had been put together for her by students from the nearby College of Art. The poems were as I remembered, but for the tone of bitterness to which I had given only passing attention when I was young.
I found myself being thankful for that, even so, because I know now that it was accurate.

Interspersed between the poems were photographs of dingy corners and brick walls, which make me think that the students who had produced Margaret's chapbook had given some thought to place and to mood in its design,

But there was one photograph of five Negro teenagers, which the students included, perhaps to offset some of the sorrow of the poems themselves, which gave me pause. I stopped reading to look closely at it, at these five young people who looked smart, ready for anything, and a bit cocky, but who were not at all out of place in a chapbook whose subject matter was city life.

That picture took me back to a night my father was building a cabinet on the kitchen table and his curses woke me. I walked into the kitchen that night on my four-year old legs. It
was going to be eight more years before my father's troubles really began, with the FBI and other people, known to me and not, but he was always a curser; he might, that night have merely hit his thumb with a hammer. I was not sure he had even seen me come in. He picked up a dowel, though, and a pair of pliers but his hands froze in midair,and he said, in his normal voice

> '*Who will carry the mail over the Hump?*'
> '*I will!*'
> '*And who are you?*'
> '*Jack Dalton!*'
> '*Not the Jack Dalton?*'
> '*Yes. Bang! Bang! Bang!*'

I remember nothing more of that night, not even how I came to be back in my bed.

When my son was four I took him into our den, the same room where we keep our books and where I had found Margaret's chapbook. I had seen Harpo Marx destroy an office filled with paper on television; it seemed like I might enjoy watching my son do it. This night I gave him a pack of five hundred three x five cards and said 'Do as you will', and it was a night when I, too, was not in the best of moods, but he threw them into the air, and I picked them all up from behind the sofa or from the overhead light or from under the bookshelves, and I asked him if he wanted to do it again and he did so I picked them up again and on and on and on until it was time for bed, time for both of us.

It is 2011 now. Margaret Levinson is gone. After I read her chapbook I looked up Jack Dalton and discovered there had been two of them, one fictional, one real. The real one did well in the Alaskan gold rush and produced a successful family. The fictional one was a character on a radio show. I can only guess which one was the subject of my father's soliloquy, I do not think it matters in the end.

Often I have told myself and others that I know nothing, really, and that is inaccurate. Often have I told myself – but not others –that I know everything, which certainly cannot be true. I try to live somewhere between these extremes. I have learned to curse even louder than my father ever could; I have also learned, I hope, how to praise. I value both; and that is an accurate statement.

I say now that *Bang! Bang! Bang!* Is still louder and more sonorous than any curse. I say I wish my son an interesting and messy life. May he have a soliloquy to tell. May he throw many things into the air! Blessings on Margaret Levinson! Blessings on both Jack Daltons! Blessings on Harpo Marx! Blessings on my father and son! Blessings on five Negro teenagers! I will have my fire escape; I will not dread it. I will insist on it. I will tell this story again

The phrases, quotes, words and sentences which served only to bring forth the present poems may be found in the following sources:

Cold Mountain Poems, Zen Poems Of Han Shan, Shih Te And Wang Fan – Shih, Tr. J.P. Seaton (Shambala, 2013);

One Hundred More Poems From The Japanese, Tr. Kenneth Rexroth (New Directions, 1976);

The Late Poems Of Wang – An –Shih, Tr. David Hinton (New Directions, 2015);

Awesome Nightfall The Life, Times And Poetry Of Saigyo, Tr. William R. LaFleur (Wisdom Books, 2003);

Essays In Idleness The Tsuruzuragusa Of Kenko, Tr. Donald Keene (Columbia University Press, 1967);

The Penguin Book Of Chinese Verse, Tr. Robert Kotewell and Norman L Smith, Penguin Books, 1962);

Written On The Sky Poems From The Japanese, Tr. Kenneth Rexroth (New Directions, 2009);

One Hundred Poems From The Japanese, Tr. Kenneth Rexroth (New Directios, 1964);

Master Sorai's Responsals An Annotated Translation of Soeri Sensei Tomonsho, Tr.Samuel Hideo Yamashita (University Of Hawaii Press, 1994);

A Hundred And Seventy Chinese Poems, Tr. Arthur Waley (Chapman Billies, Inc., 1997);

The New Directions Anthology Of Classical Chinese Poetry, Tr. William Carlos Williams, Ezra Pound, Kenneth Rexroth, Gary Snyder, David Hinton (New Directions, 2003);

The Art Of Chinese Poetry, James J.Y. Liu (University Of Chicago Press, 1962);

The Narrow Road To the Deep North And Other Travel Sketches, Tr. Nobuyuki Yuasa
(Penguin Books Ltd., 1970);

The Old Man Who Does As He Pleases Selections From The Poetry And Prose Of Lu Yu, Tr. Burton Watson (Columbia University Press, 1973);

The Late Poems Of Meng Chiao, Tr David Hinton (Princeton University Press, 1996);

Li Po And Tu Fu, Tr. Arthur Cooper (Penguin Books, 1973);

Confucianism The Analects Of Confucius, Tr. Arthur Waley (Quality Paperback Book Club, 1992).

The Rose Of Time, New and Selected Poems, Bei Dao, Tr. Yanbing Chen et al, (New Directions, 2009).